THE COMPLETE REFERENCE TO
ANGELS IN
THE BOOK OF MORMON

Also by Kermie Wohlenhaus, Ph.D.

How to Talk and Actually Listen to Your Guardian Angel
The Complete Reference to Angels in the Bible
A Quick Reference Guide to Angels in The Bible

THE COMPLETE REFERENCE TO
ANGELS IN
THE BOOK OF MORMON

Kermie Wohlenhaus, Ph.D.

KERMIE & THE ANGELS PRESS   TUCSON, ARIZONA

To contact the author or order
additional copies of this book
Kermie & The Angels Press
P. O. Box 64282
Tucson, AZ 85728
www.KermieandtheAngels.com
KermieandtheAngels@gmail.com

This edition was prepared for publication by
Ghost River Images
5350 East Fourth Street
Tucson, Arizona 85711
www.ghostriverimages.com

Cover design by Kermie Wohlenhaus

ISBN: 978-0-9832300-7-6
Library of Congress Control Number: 2014912677

Printed in the United States of America
First Printing: August, 2014
10 9 8 7 6 5 4 3 2 1

Dedicated to the Divine and the Glorious Angels

Table of Contents

ALMA

HELAMAN

3 NEPHI

MORONI

Acknowledgements   79

About The Author   80

Introduction

The Complete Reference to Angels in The Book of Mormon is an important book within the series *The Complete Reference to Angels in Sacred Texts*. This series contains the divinely guided angelic verses of many of the world's religious scriptures: *The Complete Reference to Angels in the Bible*, *The Complete Reference to Angels in The Book of Mormon*, *The Complete Reference to Angels in The Koran (Qur'an)*, and *The Complete Reference to Other Sacred Texts*. All these references are foundational texts for the field of Angelology, the study of angels.

As we read these ancient angelic scriptures, we are informed of how, even to this day, these sacred texts shape our angelic beliefs. Often, angels are overlooked and the important, intricate roles they played in ancient times go virtually unnoticed. This is why it is important to have references that focus our attention on their lifesaving, guarding, and guiding words and acts. As in ancient times, angels continue to guide us to Divine Will, if we but listen.

The Book of Mormon has over seventy-four verses regarding angels. Joseph Smith was praying to God one evening in 1823 when he had a visitation from a Being of Light who identified himself as a "messenger of God." This messenger of God identified himself further as the ascended master, Moroni. Even though it is a popular Mormon belief that Moroni was an angel, scholars continue to debate if Moroni was an enlightened ascended master or truly an angel.

Moroni revealed to Joseph Smith that he had sealed golden records many centuries prior. The messenger told Joseph Smith, in the course of three visions, that the translation tools were enclosed within these texts for interpretation. Moroni then directed Joseph to the exact location of the hiding place which was under a stone in what is now the village of Manchester, Ontario county, New York. Joseph Smith followed Moroni's instructions, found, and translated these sacred texts into what we now call "The Book of Mormon."

The Book of Mormon is said to have been originally written by several ancient writers. It documents the people of Nephi and the Lamanites, a remnant of the house of Israel. It also records their history up to the time they lived on the North American continent. These records were hidden specifically so they could be revealed to the world at the appointed time and this time was during Joseph Smith's life.

A major world religion, The Church of Jesus Christ of Latter-Day Saints (LDS), often shortened to the Mormon Church, is founded upon this sacred text, The Book of Mormon. Included within these divinely inspired pages are many diverse angel references which highlight the duties, appearance, functions, and messages of the angels to these ancient peoples. Much is added to the study of Angelology by the revelations and encounters set within this sacred text.

May the Divine guide you with inspiration and wonder as the angels within *The Book of Mormon* are revealed.

Kermie Wohlenhaus, Ph.D.
www.KermieandtheAngels.com

1 NEPHI

1 Nephi 1:8-14 - Being overcome by the Spirit in a vision, Lehi saw God sitting upon His throne, surrounded with numberless concourses of angels

1:8 And being thus overcome with the Spirit, he was carried away in a vision, even that he saw the heavens open, and he thought he saw God sitting upon his throne, surrounded with numberless concourses of <u>angels</u> in the attitude of singing and praising their God.

1:9 And it came to pass that he saw One descending out of the midst of heaven, and he beheld that his luster was above that of the sun at noon-day.

1:10 And he also saw twelve others following him, and their brightness did exceed that of the stars in the firmament.

1:11 And they came down and went forth upon the face of the earth; and the first came and stood before my father, and gave unto him a book, and bade him that he should read.

1:12 And it came to pass that as he read, he was filled with the Spirit of the Lord.

1:13 And he read, saying: Wo, wo, unto Jerusalem, for I have seen thine abominations! Yea, and many things did my father read concerning Jerusalem – that it should be destroyed, and the inhabitants thereof; many should perish by the sword, and many should be carried away captive into Babylon.

1:14 And it came to pass that when my father had read and seen many great and marvelous things, he did exclaim many things unto the Lord; such as: Great and marvelous are thy works, O Lord God Almighty! Thy throne is high in the heavens, and thy power, and goodness, and mercy are over all the inhabitants of the earth, and, because thou art merciful, thou wilt not suffer those who come unto thee that they shall perish!

1 Nephi 3:28-31 - Nephi is protected from Laman and Lemuel rod by an angel of the Lord

3:28 And it came to pass that Laman was angry with me, and also with my father; and also was Lemuel, for he hearkened unto the words of Laman. Wherefore Laman and Lemuel did speak many hard words unto us, their younger brothers, and they did smite us even with a rod.

3:29 And it came to pass as they smote us with a rod, behold, an <u>angel of the Lord</u> came and stood before them, and he spake unto them, saying: Why do ye smite your younger brother with a rod? Know ye not that the Lord hath chosen him to be a ruler over you, and this because of your iniquities? Behold ye shall go up to Jerusalem again, and the Lord will deliver Laban into your hands.

3:30 And after the <u>angel</u> had spoken unto us, he departed.

3:31 And after the <u>angel</u> had departed, Laman and Lemuel again began to murmur, saying: How is it possible that the Lord will deliver Laban into our hands? Behold, he is a mighty man, and he can command fifty, yea, even he can slay fifty; then why not us?

1 Nephi 4:2-3 - Nephi reminds brothers that an angel spoke to them

4:2 Therefore let us go up; let us be strong like unto Moses; for he truly spake unto the waters of the Red Sea and they divided hither and thither, and our fathers came through, out of captivity, on dry ground, and the armies of Pharaoh did follow and were drowned in the waters of the Red Sea.

4:3 Now behold ye know that this is true; and ye also know that an <u>angel</u> hath spoken unto you; wherefore can ye doubt? Let us go up; the Lord is able to deliver us, even as our fathers, and to destroy Laban, even as the Egyptians.

1 Nephi 7:8-10 - Nephi asking brothers how have they forgotten that they have seen an angel of the Lord

7:8 And now I, Nephi, being grieved for the hardness of their hearts, therefore I spake unto them, saying, yea, even unto Laman and unto Lemuel: Behold ye are mine elder brethren, and how is it that ye are so hard in your hearts, and so blind in your minds, that ye have need that I, your younger brother, should speak unto you, yea, and set an example for you?

7:9 How is it that ye have not hearkened unto the word of the Lord?

7:10 How is it that ye have forgotten that ye have seen an <u>angel of the Lord</u>?

1 Nephi 11:14-36 - Nephi saw the heavens open and an angel came down and he is shown a vision

11:14 And it came to pass that I saw the heavens open; and an <u>angel</u> came down and stood before me; and he said unto me: Nephi, what beholdest thou?

11:15 And I said unto him: A virgin, most beautiful and fair above all other virgins.

11:16 And he said unto me: Knowest thou the condescension of God?

11:17 And I said unto him: I know that he loveth his children; nevertheless, I do not know the meaning of all things.

11:18 And he said unto me: Behold, the virgin whom thou seest is the mother of the Son of God, after the manner of the flesh.

11:19 And it came to pass that I beheld that she was carried away in the Spirit; and after she had been carried away in the Spirit for the space of a time the <u>angel</u> spake unto me, saying: Look!

11:20 And I looked and beheld the virgin again, bearing a child in her arms.

11:21 And the <u>angel</u> said unto me: Behold the Lamb of God, yea, even the Son of the Eternal Father! Knowest thou the meaning of the tree which thy father saw?

11:22 And I answered him, saying: Yea, it is the love of God, which sheddeth itself abroad in the hearts of the children of men; wherefore, it is the most desirable above all things.

11:23 And he spake unto me, saying: Yea, and the most joyous to the soul.

11:24 And after he had said these words, he said unto me: Look! And I looked, and I beheld the Son of God going forth among the children of men; and I saw many fall down at his feet and worship him.

11:25 And it came to pass that I beheld that the rod of iron, which my father had seen, was the word of God, which led to the fountain of living waters, or to the tree of life; which waters are a representation of the love of God; and I also beheld that the tree of life was a representation of the love of God.

11:26 And the <u>angel</u> said unto me again: Look and behold the condescension of God!

11:27 And I looked and beheld the Redeemer of the world, of whom my father had spoken; and I also beheld the prophet who should prepare the way before him. And the Lamb of God went forth and was baptized of him; and after he was baptized, I beheld the heavens open, and the Holy Ghost come down out of heaven and abide upon him in the form of a dove.

11:28 And I beheld that he went forth ministering unto the people, in power and great glory; and the multitudes were gathered together to hear him; and I beheld that they cast him out from among them.

11:29 And I also beheld twelve others following him. And it came to pass that they were carried away in the Spirit from before my face, and I saw them not.

11:30 And it came to pass that the <u>angel</u> spake unto me again, saying: Look! And I looked, and I beheld the heavens open again, and I saw <u>angels</u> descending upon the children of men; and they did minister unto them.

11:31 And he spake unto me again, saying: Look! And I looked, and I beheld the Lamb of God going forth among the children of men. And I beheld multitudes of people who were sick, and who were afflicted with all manner of diseases, and with devils and unclean spirits; and the <u>angel</u> spake and showed all these things unto me. And they were healed by the power of the Lamb of God; and the devils and the unclean spirits were cast out.

11:32 And it came to pass that the <u>angel</u> spake unto me again, saying: Look! And I looked and beheld the Lamb of God, that he was taken by the people; yea, the Son of the everlasting God was judged of the world; and I saw and bear record.

11:33 And I, Nephi, saw that he was lifted up upon the cross and slain for the sins of the world.

11:34 And after he was slain I saw the multitudes of the earth, that they were gathered together to fight against the apostles of the Lamb; for thus were the twelve called by the <u>angel of the Lord</u>.

11:35 And the multitude of the earth was gathered together; and I beheld that they were in a large and spacious building, like unto the building which my father saw. And the <u>angel of the Lord</u> spake unto me again, saying: Behold the world and the wisdom thereof; yea, behold the house of Israel hath gathered together to fight against the twelve apostles of the Lamb.

11:36 And it came to pass that I saw and bear record, that the great and spacious building was the pride of the world; and it fell, and the fall thereof was exceedingly great. And the <u>angel of the Lord</u> spake unto me again, saying: Thus shall be the destruction of all nations, kindreds, tongues, and people, that shall fight against the twelve apostles of the Lamb.

1 Nephi 12:1-23 - Nephi continues with the angel vision

12:1 And it came to pass that the <u>angel</u> said unto me: Look, and behold thy seed, and also the seed of thy brethren. And I looked and beheld the land of promise; and I beheld multitudes of people, yea, even as it were in number as many as the sand of the sea.

12:2 And it came to pass that I beheld multitudes gathered together to battle, one against the other; and I beheld wars, and rumors of wars, and great slaughters with the sword among my people.

12:3 And it came to pass that I beheld many generations pass away, after the manner of wars and contentions in the land; and I beheld many cities, yea, even that I did not number them.

12:4 And it came to pass that I saw a mist of darkness on the face of the land of promise; and I saw lightnings, and I heard thunderings, and earthquakes, and all manner of tumultuous noises; and I saw the earth and the rocks, that they rent; and I saw mountains tumbling into pieces; and I saw the plains of the earth, that they were broken up; and I saw many cities that they were sunk; and I saw many that they were burned with fire; and I saw many that did tumble to the earth, because of the quaking thereof.

12:5 And it came to pass after I saw these things, I saw the vapor of darkness, that it passed from off the face of the earth; and behold, I saw multitudes who had not fallen because of the great and terrible judgments of the Lord.

12:6 And I saw the heavens open, and the Lamb of God descending out of heaven; and he came down and showed himself unto them.

12:7 And I also saw and bear record that the Holy Ghost fell upon twelve others; and they were ordained of God, and chosen.

12:8 And the <u>angel</u> spake unto me, saying: Behold the twelve disciples of the Lamb, who are chosen to minister unto thy seed.

12:9 And he said unto me: Thou rememberest the twelve apostles of the Lamb? Behold they are they who shall judge the twelve tribes of Israel; wherefore, the twelve ministers of thy seed shall be judged of them; for ye are of the house of Israel.

12:10 And these twelve ministers whom thou beholdest shall judge thy seed. And, behold, they are righteous forever; for because of their faith in the Lamb of God their garments are made white in his blood.

12:11 And the <u>angel</u> said unto me: Look! And I looked, and beheld three generations pass away in righteousness; and their garments were white even like unto the Lamb of God. And the <u>angel</u> said unto me: These are made white in the blood of the Lamb, because of their faith in him.

12:12 And I, Nephi, also saw many of the fourth generation who passed away in righteousness.

12:13 And it came to pass that I saw the multitudes of the earth gathered together.

12:14 And the <u>angel</u> said unto me: Behold thy seed, and also the seed of thy brethren.

12:15 And it came to pass that I looked and beheld the people of my seed gathered together in multitudes against the seed of my brethren; and they were gathered together to battle.

12:16 And the <u>angel</u> spake unto me, saying: Behold the fountain of filthy water which thy father saw; yea, even the river of which he spake; and the depths thereof are the depths of hell.

12:17 And the mists of darkness are the temptations of the devil, which blindeth the eyes, and hardeneth the hearts of the children of men, and leadeth them away into broad roads, that they perish and are lost.

12:18 And the large and spacious building, which thy father saw, is vain imaginations and the pride of the children of men. And a great and a terrible gulf divideth them; yea, even the word of the justice of the Eternal God, and the Messiah who is the Lamb of God, of whom the Holy Ghost beareth record, from the beginning of the world until this time, and from this time henceforth and forever.

12:19 And while the <u>angel</u> spake these words, I beheld and saw that the seed of my brethren did contend against my seed, according to the word of the angel; and because of the pride of my seed, and the temptations of the devil, I beheld that the seed of my brethren did overpower the people of my seed.

12:20 And it came to pass that I beheld, and saw the people of the seed of my brethren that they had overcome my seed; and they went forth in multitudes upon the face of the land.

12:21 And I saw them gathered together in multitudes; and I saw wars and rumors of wars among them; and in wars and rumors of wars I saw many generations pass away.

12:22 And the angel said unto me: Behold these shall dwindle in unbelief.

12:23 And it came to pass that I beheld, after they had dwindled in unbelief they became a dark, and loathsome, and a filthy people, full of idleness and all manner of abominations.

1 Nephi 13:1-42 - Nephi continues with the angel vision

13:1 And it came to pass that the angel spake unto me, saying: Look! And I looked and beheld many nations and kingdoms.

13:2 And the angel said unto me: What beholdest thou? And I said: I behold many nations and kingdoms.

13:3 And he said unto me: These are the nations and kingdoms of the Gentiles.

13:4 And it came to pass that I saw among the nations of the Gentiles the formation of a great church.

13:5 And the angel said unto me: Behold the formation of a church which is most abominable above all other churches, which slayeth the saints of God, yea, and tortureth them and bindeth them down, and yoketh them with a yoke of iron, and bringeth them down into captivity.

13:6 And it came to pass that I beheld this great and abominable church; and I saw the devil that he was the founder of it.

13:7 And I also saw gold, and silver, and silks, and scarlets, and fine-twined linen, and all manner of precious clothing; and I saw many harlots.

13:8 And the <u>angel</u> spake unto me, saying: Behold the gold, and the silver, and the silks, and the scarlets, and the fine-twined linen, and the precious clothing, and the harlots, are the desires of this great and abominable church.

13:9 And also for the praise of the world do they destroy the saints of God, and bring them down into captivity.

13:10 And it came to pass that I looked and beheld many waters; and they divided the Gentiles from the seed of my brethren.

13:11 And it came to pass that the <u>angel</u> said unto me: Behold the wrath of God is upon the seed of thy brethren.

13:12 And I looked and beheld a man among the Gentiles, who was separated from the seed of my brethren by the many waters; and I beheld the Spirit of God, that it came down and wrought upon the man; and he went forth upon the many waters, even unto the seed of my brethren, who were in the promised land.

13:13 And it came to pass that I beheld the Spirit of God, that it wrought upon other Gentiles; and they went forth out of captivity, upon the many waters.

13:14 And it came to pass that I beheld many multitudes of the Gentiles upon the land of promise; and I beheld the wrath of God, that it was upon the seed of my brethren; and they were scattered before the Gentiles and were smitten.

13:15 And I beheld the Spirit of the Lord, that it was upon the Gentiles, and they did prosper and obtain the land for their inheritance; and I beheld that they were white, and exceedingly fair and beautiful, like unto my people before they were slain.

13:16 And it came to pass that I, Nephi, beheld that the Gentiles who had gone forth out of captivity did humble themselves before the Lord; and the power of the Lord was with them.

13:17 And I beheld that their mother Gentiles were gathered together upon the waters, and upon the land also, to battle against them.

13:18 And I beheld that the power of God was with them, and also that the wrath of God was upon all those that were gathered together against them to battle.

13:19 And I, Nephi, beheld that the Gentiles that had gone out of captivity were delivered by the power of God out of the hands of all other nations.

13:20 And it came to pass that I, Nephi, beheld that they did prosper in the land; and I beheld a book, and it was carried forth among them.

13:21 And the <u>angel</u> said unto me: Knowest thou the meaning of the book?

13:22 And I said unto him: I know not.

13:23 And he said: Behold it proceedeth out of the mouth of a Jew. And I, Nephi, beheld it; and he said unto me: The book that thou beholdest is a record of the Jews, which contains the covenants of the Lord, which he hath made unto the house of Israel; and it also containeth many of the prophecies of the holy prophets; and it is a record like unto the engravings which are upon the plates of brass, save there are not so many; nevertheless, they contain the covenants of the Lord, which he hath made unto the house of Israel; wherefore, they are of great worth unto the Gentiles.

13:24 And the <u>angel of the Lord</u> said unto me: Thou hast beheld that the book proceeded forth from the mouth of a Jew; and when it proceeded forth from the mouth of a Jew it contained the fulness of the gospel of the Lord, of whom the twelve apostles bear record; and they bear record according to the truth which is in the Lamb of God.

13:25 Wherefore, these things go forth from the Jews in purity unto the Gentiles, according to the truth which is in God.

13:26 And after they go forth by the hand of the twelve apostles of the Lamb, from the Jews unto the Gentiles, thou seest the formation of a great and abominable church, which is most abominable above all other churches; for behold, they have taken away from the gospel of the Lamb many parts which are plain and most precious; and also many covenants of the Lord have they taken away.

13:27 And all this have they done that they might pervert the right ways of the Lord, that they might blind the eyes and harden the hearts of the children of men.

13:28 Wherefore, thou seest that after the book hath gone forth through the hands of the great and abominable church, that there are many plain and precious things taken away from the book, which is the book of the Lamb of God.

13:29 And after these plain and precious things were taken away it goeth forth unto all the nations of the Gentiles; and after it goeth forth unto all the nations of the Gentiles, yea, even across the many waters which thou hast seen with the Gentiles which have gone forth out of captivity, thou seest – because of the many plain and precious things which have been taken out of the book, which were plain unto the understanding of the children of men, according to the plainness which is in the Lamb of God – because of these things which are taken away out of the gospel of the Lamb, an exceedingly great many do stumble, yea, insomuch that Satan hath great power over them.

13:30 Nevertheless, thou beholdest that the Gentiles who have gone forth out of captivity, and have been lifted up by the power of God above all other nations, upon the face of the land which is choice above all other lands, which is the land that the Lord God hath covenanted with thy father that his seed should have for the land of their inheritance; wherefore, thou seest that the Lord God will not suffer that the Gentiles will utterly destroy the mixture of thy seed, which are among thy brethren.

13:31 Neither will he suffer that the Gentiles shall destroy the seed of thy brethren.

13:32 Neither will the Lord God suffer that the Gentiles shall forever remain in that awful state of blindness, which thou beholdest they are in, because of the plain and most precious parts of the gospel of the Lamb which have been kept back by that abominable church, whose formation thou hast seen.

13:33 Wherefore saith the Lamb of God: I will be merciful unto the Gentiles, unto the visiting of the remnant of the house of Israel in great judgment.

13:34 And it came to pass that the angel of the Lord spake unto me, saying: Behold, saith the Lamb of God, after I have visited the remnant of the house of Israel – and this remnant of whom I speak is the seed of thy father – wherefore, after I have visited them in judgment, and smitten them by the hand of the Gentiles, and after the Gentiles do stumble exceedingly, because of the most plain and precious parts of the gospel of the Lamb which have been kept back by that abominable church, which is the mother of harlots, saith the Lamb – I will be merciful unto the Gentiles in that day, insomuch that I will bring forth unto them, in mine own power, much of my gospel, which shall be plain and precious, saith the Lamb.

13:35 For, behold, saith the Lamb: I will manifest myself unto thy seed, that they shall write many things which I shall minister unto them, which shall be plain and precious; and after thy seed shall be destroyed, and dwindle in unbelief, and also the seed of thy brethren, behold, these things shall be hid up, to come forth unto the Gentiles, by the gift and power of the Lamb.

13:36 And in them shall be written my gospel, saith the Lamb, and my rock and my salvation.

13:37 And blessed are they who shall seek to bring forth my Zion at that day, for they shall have the gift and the power of the Holy Ghost; and if they endure unto the end they shall be lifted up at the last day, and shall be saved in the everlasting kingdom of the Lamb; and whoso shall publish peace, yea, tidings of great joy, how beautiful upon the mountains shall they be.

13:38 And it came to pass that I beheld the remnant of the seed of my brethren, and also the book of the Lamb of God, which had proceeded forth from the mouth of the Jew, that it came forth from the Gentiles unto the remnant of the seed of my brethren.

13:39 And after it had come forth unto them I beheld other books, which came forth by the power of the Lamb, from the Gentiles unto them, unto the convincing of the Gentiles and the remnant of the seed of my brethren, and also the Jews who were scattered upon all the face of the earth, that the records of the prophets and of the twelve apostles of the Lamb are true.

13:40 And the <u>angel</u> spake unto me, saying: These last records, which thou hast seen among the Gentiles, shall establish the truth of the first, which are of the twelve apostles of the Lamb, and shall make known the plain and precious things which have been taken away from them; and shall make known to all kindreds, tongues, and people, that the Lamb of God is the Son of the Eternal Father, and the Savior of the world; and that all men must come unto him, or they cannot be saved.

13:41 And they must come according to the words which shall be established by the mouth of the Lamb; and the words of the Lamb shall be made known in the records of thy seed, as well as in the records of the twelve apostles of the Lamb; wherefore they both shall be established in one; for there is one God and one Shepherd over all the earth.

13:42 And the time cometh that he shall manifest himself unto all nations, both unto the Jews and also unto the Gentiles; and after he has manifested himself unto the Jews and also unto the Gentiles, then he shall manifest himself unto the Gentiles and also unto the Jews, and the last shall be first, and the first shall be last.

1 Nephi 14:5-30 - Nephi continues with the angel vision

14:5 And it came to pass that the angel spake unto me, Nephi, saying: Thou hast beheld that if the Gentiles repent it shall be well with them; and thou also knowest concerning the covenants of the Lord unto the house of Israel; and thou also hast heard that whoso repenteth not must perish.

14:6 Therefore, wo be unto the Gentiles if it so be that they harden their hearts against the Lamb of God.

14:7 For the time cometh, saith the Lamb of God, that I will work a great and a marvelous work among the children of men; a work which shall be everlasting, either on the one hand or on the other – either to the convincing of them unto peace and life eternal, or unto the deliverance of them to the hardness of their hearts and the blindness of their minds unto their being brought down into captivity, and also into destruction, both temporally and spiritually, according to the captivity of the devil, of which I have spoken.

14:8 And it came to pass that when the angel had spoken these words, he said unto me: Rememberest thou the covenants of the Father unto the house of Israel? I said unto him, Yea.

14:9 And it came to pass that he said unto me: Look, and behold that great and abominable church, which is the mother of abominations, whose founder is the devil.

14:10 And he said unto me: Behold there are save two churches only; the one is the church of the Lamb of God, and the other is the church of the devil; wherefore, whoso belongeth not to the church of the Lamb of God belongeth to that great church, which is the mother of abominations; and she is the whore of all the earth.

14:11 And it came to pass that I looked and beheld the whore of all the earth, and she sat upon many waters; and she had dominion over all the earth, among all nations, kindreds, tongues, and people.

14:12 And it came to pass that I beheld the church of the Lamb of God, and its numbers were few, because of the wickedness and abominations of the whore who sat upon many waters; nevertheless, I beheld that the church of the Lamb, who were the saints of God, were also upon all the face of the earth; and their dominions upon the face of the earth were small, because of the wickedness of the great whore whom I saw.

14:13 And it came to pass that I beheld that the great mother of abominations did gather together multitudes upon the face of all the earth, among all the nations of the Gentiles, to fight against the Lamb of God.

14:14 And it came to pass that I, Nephi, beheld the power of the Lamb of God, that it descended upon the saints of the church of the Lamb, and upon the covenant people of the Lord, who were scattered upon all the face of the earth; and they were armed with righteousness and with the power of God in great glory.

14:15 And it came to pass that I beheld that the wrath of God was poured out upon that great and abominable church, insomuch that there were wars and rumors of wars among all the nations and kindreds of the earth.

14:16 And as there began to be wars and rumors of wars among all the nations which belonged to the mother of abominations, the angel spake unto me, saying: Behold, the wrath of God is upon the mother of harlots; and behold, thou seest all these things –

14:17 And when the day cometh that the wrath of God is poured out upon the mother of harlots, which is the great and abominable church of all the earth, whose founder is the devil, then, at that day, the work of the Father shall commence, in preparing the way for the fulfilling of his covenants, which he hath made to his people who are of the house of Israel.

14:18 And it came to pass that the <u>angel</u> spake unto me, saying: Look!

14:19 And I looked and beheld a man, and he was dressed in a white robe.

14:20 And the <u>angel</u> said unto me: Behold one of the twelve apostles of the Lamb.

14:21 Behold, he shall see and write the remainder of these things; yea, and also many things which have been.

14:22 And he shall also write concerning the end of the world.

14:23 Wherefore, the things which he shall write are just and true; and behold they are written in the book which thou beheld proceeding out of the mouth of the Jew; and at the time they proceeded out of the mouth of the Jew, or, at the time the book proceeded out of the mouth of the Jew, the things which were written were plain and pure, and most precious and easy to the understanding of all men.

12:24 And behold, the things which this apostle of the Lamb shall write are many things which thou hast seen; and behold, the remainder shalt thou see.

12:25 But the things which thou shalt see hereafter thou shalt not write; for the Lord God hath ordained the apostle of the Lamb of God that he should write them.

12:26 And also others who have been, to them hath he shown all things, and they have written them; and they are sealed up to come forth in their purity, according to the truth which is in the Lamb, in the own due time of the Lord, unto the house of Israel.

12:27 And I, Nephi, heard and bear record, that the name of the apostle of the Lamb was John, according to the word of the <u>angel</u>.

12:28 And behold, I, Nephi, am forbidden that I should write the remainder of the things which I saw and heard; wherefore the things which I have written sufficeth me; and I have written but a small part of the things which I saw.

12:29 And I bear record that I saw the things which my father saw, and the <u>angel of the Lord</u> did make them known unto me.

12:30 And now I make an end of speaking concerning the things which I saw while I was carried away in the spirit; and if all the things which I saw are not written, the things which I have written are true. And thus it is. Amen.

1 Nephi 15:28-30 - Nephi tells his brothers of the vision and interpretation of their father's dream by the angel

15:28 And I said unto them that it was an awful gulf, which separated the wicked from the tree of life, and also from the saints of God.

15:29 And I said unto them that it was a representation of that awful hell, which the <u>angel</u> said unto me was prepared for the wicked.

15:30 And I said unto them that our father also saw that the justice of God did also divide the wicked from the righteous; and the brightness thereof was like unto the brightness of a flaming fire, which ascendeth up unto God forever and ever, and hath no end.

1 Nephi 16:37-38 - Brothers say that Nephi lied about the angels

16:37 And Laman said unto Lemuel and also unto the sons of Ishmael: Behold, let us slay our father, and also our brother Nephi, who has taken it upon him to be our ruler and our teacher, who are his elder brethren.

16:38 Now, he says that the Lord has talked with him, and also that <u>angels</u> have ministered unto him. But behold, we know that he lies unto us; and he tells us these things, and he worketh many things by his cunning arts, that he may deceive our eyes, thinking, perhaps, that he may lead us away into some strange wilderness; and after he has led us away, he has thought to make himself a king and a ruler over us, that he may do with us according to his will and pleasure. And after this manner did my brother Laman stir up their hearts to anger.

1 Nephi 17:44-45 - Nephi reminds his rebellious brothers about angel

17:44 Wherefore, the Lord commanded my father that he should depart into the wilderness; and the Jews also sought to take away his life; yea, and ye also have sought to take away his life; wherefore, ye are murderers in your hearts and ye are like unto them.

17:45 Ye are swift to do iniquity but slow to remember the Lord your God. Ye have seen an <u>angel</u>, and he spake unto you; yea, ye have heard his voice from time to time; and he hath spoken unto you in a still small voice, but ye were past feeling, that ye could not feel his words; wherefore, he has spoken unto you like unto the voice of thunder, which did cause the earth to shake as if it were to divide asunder.

1 Nephi 19:6-10 - Angel tells Nephi that God of Israel will come 600 years after Lehi left Jerusalem

19:6 Nevertheless, I do not write anything upon plates save it be that I think it be sacred. And now, if I do err, even did they err of old; not that I would excuse myself because of other men, but because of the weakness which is in me, according to the flesh, I would excuse myself.

19:7 For the things which some men esteem to be of great worth, both to the body and soul, others set at naught and trample under their feet. Yea, even the very God of Israel do men trample under their feet; I say, trample under their feet but I would speak in other words – they set him at naught, and hearken not to the voice of his counsels.

19:8 And behold he cometh, according to the words of the <u>angel</u>, in six hundred years from the time my father left Jerusalem.

19:9 And the world, because of their iniquity, shall judge him to be a thing of naught; wherefore they scourge him, and he suffereth it; and they smite him, and he suffereth it. Yea, they spit upon him, and he suffereth it, because of his loving kindness and his long-suffering towards the children of men.

19:10 And the God of our fathers, who were led out of Egypt, out of bondage, and also were preserved in the wilderness by him, yea, the God of Abraham, and of Isaac, and the God of Jacob, yieldeth himself, according to the words of the <u>angel</u>, as a man, into the hands of wicked men, to be lifted up, according to the words of Zenock, and to be crucified, according to the words of Neum, and to be buried in a sepulchre, according to the words of Zenos, which he spake concerning the three days of darkness, which should be a sign given of his death unto those who should inhabit the isles of the sea, more especially given unto those who are of the house of Israel.

2 NEPHI

2 Nephi 2:17-20 - Lehi speaks to his sons about an angel of God falling and becoming a devil

2:17 And I, Lehi, according to the things which I have read, must needs suppose that an <u>angel of God</u>, according to that which is written, had fallen from heaven; wherefore, he became a devil, having sought that which was evil before God.

2:18 And because he had fallen from heaven, and had become miserable forever, he sought also the misery of all mankind. Wherefore, he said unto Eve, yea, even that old serpent, who is the devil, who is the father of all lies, wherefore he said: Partake of the forbidden fruit, and ye shall not die, but ye shall be as God, knowing good and evil.

2:19 And after Adam and Eve had partaken of the forbidden fruit they were driven out of the garden of Eden, to till the earth.

2:20 And they have brought forth children; yea, even the family of all the earth.

2 Nephi 4:20-25 - Nephi tells how angels ministered to him

4:20 My God hath been my support; he hath led me through mine afflictions in the wilderness; and he hath preserved me upon the waters of the great deep.

4:21 He hath filled me with his love, even unto the consuming of my flesh.

4:22 He hath confounded mine enemies, unto the causing of them to quake before me.

4:23 Behold, he hath heard my cry by day, and he hath given me knowledge by visions in the nighttime.

4:24 And by day have I waxed bold in mighty prayer before him; yea, my voice have I sent up on high; and <u>angels</u> came down and ministered unto me.

4:25 And upon the wings of his Spirit hath my body been carried away upon exceedingly high mountains. And mine eyes have beheld great things, yea, even too great for man; therefore I was bidden that I should not write them.

2 Nephi 6:8-18 - Jacob recounts what the angel said to him about the Holy One of Israel

6:8 And now I, Jacob, would speak somewhat concerning these words. For behold, the Lord has shown me that those who were at Jerusalem, from whence we came, have been slain and carried away captive.

6:9 Nevertheless, the Lord has shown unto me that they should return again. And he also has shown unto me that the Lord God, the Holy One of Israel, should manifest himself unto them in the flesh; and after he should manifest himself they should scourge him and crucify him, according to the words of the <u>angel</u> who spake it unto me.

6:10 And after they have hardened their hearts and stiffened their necks against the Holy One of Israel, behold the judgments of the Holy One of Israel shall come upon them. And the day cometh that they shall be smitten and afflicted.

6:11 Wherefore, after they are driven to and fro, for thus saith the <u>angel</u>, many shall be afflicted in the flesh, and shall not be suffered to perish, because of the prayers of the faithful; they shall be scattered, and smitten, and hated; nevertheless, the Lord will be merciful unto them, that when they shall come to the knowledge of their Redeemer, they shall be gathered together again to the lands of their inheritance.

6:12 And blessed are the Gentiles, they of whom the prophet has written; for behold, if it so be that they shall repent and fight not against Zion, and do not unite themselves to that great and abominable church, they shall be saved; for the Lord God will fulfil his covenants which he has made unto his children; and for this cause the prophet has written these things.

6:13 Wherefore, they that fight against Zion and the covenant people of the Lord shall lick up the dust of their feet; and the people of the Lord shall not be ashamed. For the people of the Lord are they who wait for him; for they still wait for the coming of the Messiah.

6:14 And behold, according to the words of the prophet, the Messiah will set himself again the second time to recover them; wherefore, he will manifest himself unto them in power and great glory, unto the destruction of their enemies, when that day cometh when they shall believe in him; and none will he destroy that believe in him.

6:15 And they that believe not in him shall be destroyed, both by fire, and by tempest, and by earthquakes, and by bloodsheds, and by pestilence, and by famine. And they shall know that the Lord is God, the Holy One of Israel.

6:16 For shall the prey be taken from the mighty, or the lawful captive delivered?

6:17 But thus saith the Lord: Even the captives of the mighty shall be taken away, and the prey of the terrible shall be delivered; for the Mighty God shall deliver his covenant people. For thus saith the Lord: I will contend with them that contendeth with thee –

6:18 And I will feed them that oppress thee, with their own flesh; and they shall be drunken with their own blood as with sweet wine; and all flesh shall know that I the Lord am thy Savior and thy Redeemer, the Mighty One of Jacob.

2 Nephi 9:8-9 - The angel who fell and became the devil

9:8 O the wisdom of God, his mercy and grace! For behold, if the flesh should rise no more our spirits must become subject to that <u>angel</u> who fell from before the presence of the Eternal God, and became the devil, to rise no more.

9:9 And our spirits must have become like unto him, and we become devils, <u>angels</u> to a devil, to be shut out from the presence of our God, and to remain with the father of lies, in misery, like unto himself; yea, to that being who beguiled our first parents, who transformeth himself nigh unto an angel of light, and stirreth up the children of men unto secret combinations of murder and all manner of secret works of darkness.

2 Nephi 9:16 - The devil and his angels shall go away into everlasting fire and torment as fire and brimstone

9:16 And assuredly, as the Lord liveth, for the Lord God hath spoken it, and it is his eternal word, which cannot pass away, that they who are righteous shall be righteous still, and they who are filthy shall be filthy still; wherefore, they who are filthy are the devil and his <u>angels</u>; and they shall go away into everlasting fire; prepared for them; and their torment is as a lake of fire and brimstone, whose flame ascendeth up forever and ever and has no end.

2 Nephi 10:1-4 - Jacob speaks of an angel who tells him about Christ's coming and crucifixion

10:1 And now I, Jacob, speak unto you again, my beloved brethren, concerning this righteous branch of which I have spoken.

10:2 For behold, the promises which we have obtained are promises unto us according to the flesh; wherefore, as it has been shown unto me that many of our children shall perish in the flesh because of unbelief, nevertheless, God will be merciful unto many; and our children shall be restored, that they may come to that which will give them the true knowledge of their Redeemer.

10:3 Wherefore, as I said unto you, it must needs be expedient that Christ – for in the last night the <u>angel</u> spake unto me that this should be his name – should come among the Jews, among those who are the more wicked part of the world; and they shall crucify him – for thus it behooveth our God, and there is none other nation on earth that would crucify their God.

10:4 For should the mighty miracles be wrought among other nations they would repent, and know that he be their God.

2 Nephi 16:1-7 - Isaiah sees the Seraphim and describes them

16:1 In the year that king Uzziah died, I saw also the Lord sitting upon a throne, high and lifted up, and his train filled the temple.

16:2 Above it stood the <u>seraphim</u>; each one had six wings; with twain he covered his face, and with twain he covered his feet, and with twain he did fly.

16:3 And one cried unto another, and said: Holy, holy, holy, is the Lord of Hosts; the whole earth is full of his glory. ,

16:4 And the posts of the door moved at the voice of him that cried, and the house was filled with smoke.

16:5 Then said I: Wo is unto me! for I am undone; because I am a man of unclean lips; and I dwell in the midst of a people of unclean lips; for mine eyes have seen the King, the Lord of Hosts.

16:6 Then flew one of the <u>seraphim</u> unto me, having a live coal in his hand, which he had taken with the tongs from off the altar;

16:7 And he laid it upon my mouth, and said: Lo, this has touched thy lips; and thine iniquity is taken away, and thy sin purged.

2 Nephi 25:17-19 - Angel of God says that the Messiah's name is Jesus Christ, the Son of God

25:17 And the Lord will set his hand again the second time to restore his people from their lost and fallen state. Wherefore, he will proceed to do a marvelous work and a wonder among the children of men.

25:18 Wherefore, he shall bring forth his words unto them, which words shall judge them at the last day, for they shall be given them for the purpose of convincing them of the true Messiah, who was rejected by them; and unto the convincing of them that they need not look forward any more for a Messiah to come, for there should not any come, save it should be a false Messiah which should deceive the people; for there is save one Messiah spoken of by the prophets, and that Messiah is he who should be rejected of the Jews.

25:19 For according to the words of the prophets, the Messiah cometh in six hundred years from the time that my father left Jerusalem; and according to the words of the prophets, and also the word of the <u>angel of God</u>, his name shall be Jesus Christ, the Son of God.

2 Nephi 31:13-14 - Nephi speaks of receiving the Holy Ghost with the baptism of fire and then speaks with the tongue of angels

31:13 Wherefore, my beloved brethren, I know that if ye shall follow the Son, with full purpose of heart, acting no hypocrisy and no deception before God, but with real intent, repenting of your sins, witnessing unto the Father that ye are willing to take upon you the name of Christ, by baptism – yea, by following your Lord and your Savior down into the water, according to his word, behold, then shall ye receive the Holy Ghost; yea, then cometh the baptism of fire and of the Holy Ghost; and then can ye speak with the tongue of <u>angels</u>, and shout praises unto the Holy One of Israel.

13:14 But, behold, my beloved brethren, thus came the voice of the Son unto me, saying: After ye have repented of your sins, and witnessed unto the Father that ye are willing to keep my commandments, by the baptism of water, and have received the baptism of fire and of the Holy Ghost, and can speak with a new tongue, yea, even with the tongue of <u>angels</u>, and after this should deny me, it would have been better for you that ye had not known me.

2 Nephi 32:1-5 - Nephi tells that after receiving the Holy Ghost ye can speak with the tongue of angels

32:1 And now, behold, my beloved brethren, I suppose that ye ponder somewhat in your hearts concerning that which ye should do after ye have entered in by the way. But, behold, why do ye ponder these things in your hearts?

32:2 Do ye not remember that I said unto you that after ye had received the Holy Ghost ye could speak with the tongue of <u>angels</u>?

And now, how could ye speak with the tongue of <u>angels</u> save it were by the Holy Ghost?

32:3 Angels speak by the power of the Holy Ghost; wherefore, they speak the words of Christ. Wherefore, I said unto you, feast upon the words of Christ; for behold, the words of Christ will tell you all things what ye should do.

32:4 Wherefore, now after I have spoken these words, if ye cannot understand them it will be because ye ask not, neither do ye knock; wherefore, ye are not brought into the light, but must perish in the dark.

32:5 For behold, again I say unto you that if ye will enter in by the way, and receive the Holy Ghost, it will show unto you all things what ye should do.

JACOB

Jacob 3:11 - Jacob says to hearken unto my words that ye may not become angels to the devil

3:11 O my brethren, hearken unto my words; arouse the faculties of your souls; shake yourselves that ye may awake from the slumber of death; and loose yourselves from the pains of hell that ye may not become <u>angels</u> to the devil, to be cast into that lake of fire and brimstone which is the second death.

Jacob 7:1-5 - Jacob says he had truly seen angels and they ministered unto him

7:1 And now it came to pass after some years had passed away, there came a man among the people of Nephi, whose name was Sherem.

7:2 And it came to pass that he began to preach among the people, and to declare unto them that there should be no Christ. And he preached many things which were flattering unto the people; and this he did that he might overthrow the doctrine of Christ.

7:3 And he labored diligently that he might lead away the hearts of the people, insomuch that he did lead away many hearts; and he knowing that I, Jacob, had faith in Christ who should come, he sought much opportunity that he might come unto me.

7:4 And he was learned, that he had a perfect knowledge of the language of the people; wherefore, he could use much flattery, and much power of speech, according to the power of the devil.

7:5 And he had hope to shake me from the faith, notwithstanding the many revelations and the many things which I had seen concerning these things; for I truly had seen <u>angels,</u> and they had ministered unto me. And also, I had heard the voice of the Lord speaking unto me in very word, from time to time; wherefore, I could not be shaken.

Jacob 7:16-17 - Jacob speaks plainly about the power of the Holy Ghost and the ministering of angels

7:16 And it came to pass that he said unto the people: Gather together on the morrow, for I shall die; wherefore, I desire to speak unto the people before I shall die.

7:17 And it came to pass that on the morrow the multitude were gathered together; and he spake plainly unto them and denied the things which he had taught them, and confessed the Christ, and the power of the Holy Ghost, and the ministering of <u>angels.</u>

OMNI

Omni 1:23-25 - Amaleke speaks to the belief of ministering of angels

1:23 Behold, I, Amaleki, was born in the days of Mosiah; and I have lived to see his death; and Benjamin, his son, reigneth in his stead.

1:24 And behold, I have seen, in the days of king Benjamin, a serious war and much bloodshed between the Nephites and the Lamanites. But behold, the Nephites did obtain much advantage over them; yea, insomuch that king Benjamin did drive them out of the land of Zarahemla.

1:25 And it came to pass that I began to be old; and, having no seed, and knowing king Benjamin to be a just man before the Lord, wherefore, I shall deliver up these plates unto him, exhorting all men to come unto God, the Holy One of Israel, and believe in prophesying, and in revelations, and in the ministering of <u>angels</u>, and in the gift of speaking with tongues, and in the gift of interpreting languages, and in all things which are good; for there is nothing which is good save it comes from the Lord; and that which is evil cometh from the devil.

MOSIAH

Mosiah 3:1-27 - King Benjamin speaks about the things an angel from God made known to him

3:1 And again my brethren, I would call your attention, for I have somewhat more to speak unto you; for behold, I have things to tell you concerning that which is to come.

3:2 And the things which I shall tell you are made known unto me by an <u>angel from God</u>. And he said unto me: Awake; and I awoke, and behold he stood before me.

3:3 And he said unto me: Awake, and hear the words which I shall tell thee; for behold, I am come to declare unto you the glad tidings of great joy.

3:4 For the Lord hath heard thy prayers, and hath judged of thy righteousness, and hath sent me to declare unto thee that thou mayest rejoice; and that thou mayest declare unto thy people, that they may also be filled with joy.

3:5 For behold, the time cometh, and is not far distant, that with power, the Lord Omnipotent who reigneth, who was, and is from all eternity to all eternity, shall come down from heaven among the children of men, and shall dwell in a tabernacle of clay, and shall go forth amongst men, working mighty miracles, such as healing the sick, raising the dead, causing the lame to walk, the blind to receive their sight, and the deaf to hear, and curing all manner of diseases.

3:6 And he shall cast out devils, or the evil spirits which dwell in the hearts of the children of men.

3:7 And lo, he shall suffer temptations, and pain of body, hunger, thirst, and fatigue, even more than man can suffer, except it be unto death; for behold, blood cometh from every pore, so great shall be his anguish for the wickedness and the abominations of his people.

3:8 And he shall be called Jesus Christ, the Son of God, the Father of heaven and earth, the Creator of all things from the beginning; and his mother shall be called Mary.

3:9 And lo, he cometh unto his own, that salvation might come unto the children of men even through faith on his name; and even after all this they shall consider him a man, and say that he hath a devil, and shall scourge him, and shall crucify him.

3:10 And he shall rise the third day from the dead; and behold, he standeth to judge the world; and behold, all these things are done that a righteous judgment might come upon the children of men.

3:11 For behold, and also his blood atoneth for the sins of those who have fallen by the transgression of Adam, who have died not knowing the will of God concerning them, or who have ignorantly sinned.

3:12 But wo, wo unto him who knoweth that he rebelleth against God! For salvation cometh to none such except it be through repentance and faith on the Lord Jesus Christ.

3:13 And the Lord God hath sent his holy prophets among all the children of men, to declare these things to every kindred, nation, and tongue, that thereby whosoever should believe that Christ should come, the same might receive remission of their sins, and rejoice with exceedingly great joy, even as though he had already come among them.

3:14 Yet the Lord God saw that his people were a stiffnecked people, and he appointed unto them a law, even the law of Moses.

3:15 And many signs, and wonders, and types, and shadows showed he unto them, concerning his coming; and also holy prophets spake unto them concerning his coming; and yet they hardened their hearts, and understood not that the law of Moses availeth nothing except it were through the atonement of his blood.

3:16 And even if it were possible that little children could sin they could not be saved; but I say unto you they are blessed; for behold, as in Adam, or by nature, they fall, even so the blood of Christ atoneth for their sins.

3:17 And moreover, I say unto you, that there shall be no other name given nor any other way nor means whereby salvation can come unto the children of men, only in and through the name of Christ, the Lord Omnipotent.

3:18 For behold he judgeth, and his judgment is just; and the infant perisheth not that dieth in his infancy; but men drink damnation to their own souls except they humble themselves and become as little children, and believe that salvation was, and is, and is to come, in and through the atoning blood of Christ, the Lord Omnipotent.

3:19 For the natural man is an enemy to God, and has been from the fall of Adam, and will be, forever and ever, unless he yields to the enticings of the Holy Spirit, and putteth off the natural man and becometh a saint through the atonement of Christ the Lord, and becometh as a child, submissive, meek, humble, patient, full of love, willing to submit to all things which the Lord seeth fit to inflict upon him, even as a child doth submit to his father.

3:20 And moreover, I say unto you, that the time shall come when the knowledge of the Savior shall spread throughout every nation, kindred, tongue, and people.

3:21 And behold, when that time cometh, none shall be found blameless before God, except it be little children, only through repentance and faith on the name of the Lord God Omnipotent.

3:22 And even at this time, when thou shalt have taught thy people the things which the Lord thy God hath commanded thee, even then are they found no more blameless in the sight of God, only according to the words which I have spoken unto thee.

3:23 And now I have spoken the words which the Lord God hath commanded me.

3:24 And thus saith the Lord: They shall stand as a bright testimony against this people, at the judgment day; whereof they shall be judged, every man according to his works, whether they be good, or whether they be evil.

3:25 And if they be evil they are consigned to an awful view of their own guilt and abominations, which doth cause them to shrink from the presence of the Lord into a state of misery and endless torment, from whence they can no more return; therefore they have drunk damnation to their own souls.

3:26 Therefore, they have drunk out of the cup of the wrath of God, which justice could no more deny unto them than it could deny that Adam should fall because of his partaking of the forbidden fruit; therefore, mercy could have claim on them no more forever.

3:27 And their torment is as a lake of fire and brimstone, whose flames are unquenchable, and whose smoke ascendeth up forever and ever. Thus hath the Lord commanded me. Amen.

Mosiah 4:1 - King Benjamin speaking and the words which had been delivered unto him by an angel of the Lord

4:1 And now, it came to pass that when king Benjamin had made an end of speaking the words which had been delivered unto him by the angel of the Lord, that he cast his eyes round about on the multitude, and behold they had fallen to the earth, for the fear of the Lord had come upon them.

Mosiah 4:11 - King Benjamin again recounts that which is to come which was spoken by the mouth of the angel

4:11 And again I say unto you as I have said before, that as ye have come to the knowledge of the glory of God, or if ye have known of his goodness and have tasted of his love, and have received a remission of your sins, which causeth such exceedingly great joy in your souls, even so I would that ye should remember, and always retain in remembrance, the greatness of God, and your own nothingness, and his goodness and long-suffering towards you, unworthy creatures, and humble yourselves even in the depths of humility, calling on the name of the Lord daily, and standing steadfastly in the faith of that which is to come, which was spoken by the mouth of the angel.

Mosiah 5:1-6 - King Benjamin refers to the covenant of God and obeying commandments or bringing upon themselves the never ending torment as was spoken by the angel

5:1 And now, it came to pass that when king Benjamin had thus spoken to his people, he sent among them, desiring to know of his people if they believed the words which he had spoken unto them.

5:2 And they all cried with one voice, saying: Yea, we believe all the words which thou hast spoken unto us; and also, we know of their surety and truth, because of the Spirit of the Lord Omnipotent, which has wrought a mighty change in us, or in our hearts, that we have no more disposition to do evil, but to do good continually.

5:3 And we, ourselves, also, through the infinite goodness of God, and the manifestations of his Spirit, have great views of that which is to come; and were it expedient, we could prophesy of all things.

5:4 And it is the faith which we have had on the things which our king has spoken unto us that has brought us to this great knowledge, whereby we do rejoice with such exceedingly great joy.

5:5 And we are willing to enter into a covenant with our God to do his will, and to be obedient to his commandments in all things that he shall command us, all the remainder of our days, that we may not bring upon ourselves a never-ending torment, as has been spoken by the angel, that we may not drink out of the cup of the wrath of God.

5:6 And now, these are the words which king Benjamin desired of them; and therefore he said unto them: Ye have spoken the words that I desired; and the covenant which ye have made is a righteous covenant.

Mosiah 26:24-27 - God talks to Alma about the second trump sounding and the everlasting fire prepared by the devil and his angels

26:24 For behold, in my name are they called; and if they know me they shall come forth, and shall have a place eternally at my right hand.

26:25 And it shall come to pass that when the second trump shall sound then shall they that never knew me come forth and shall stand before me.

26:26 And then shall they know that I am the Lord their God, that I am their Redeemer; but they would not be redeemed.

26:27 And then I will confess unto them that I never knew them; and they shall depart into everlasting fire prepared for the devil and his angels.

Mosiah 27:10-20 - Alma the younger and four sons of Mosiah seek to destroy the church but an angel of the Lord appears and stops them and his voice was as thunder which shook the earth

27:10 And now it came to pass that while he was going about to destroy the church of God, for he did go about secretly with the sons of Mosiah seeking to destroy the church, and to lead astray the people of the Lord, contrary to the commandments of God, or even the king –

27:11 And as I said unto you, as they were going about rebelling against God, behold, the angel of the Lord appeared unto them; and he descended as it were in a cloud; and he spake as it were with a voice of thunder, which caused the earth to shake upon which they stood;

27:12 And so great was their astonishment, that they fell to the earth, and understood not the words which he spake unto them.

27:13 Nevertheless he cried again, saying: Alma, arise and stand forth, for why persecutest thou the church of God? For the Lord hath said: This is my church, and I will establish it; and nothing shall overthrow it, save it is the transgression of my people.

27:14 And again, the angel said: Behold, the Lord hath heard the prayers of his people, and also the prayers of his servant, Alma, who is thy father; for he has prayed with much faith concerning thee that thou mightest be brought to the knowledge of the truth; therefore, for this purpose have I come to convince thee of the power and authority of God, that the prayers of his servants might be answered according to their faith.

27:15 And now behold, can ye dispute the power of God? For behold, doth not my voice shake the earth? And can ye not also behold me before you? And I am sent from God.

27:16 Now I say unto thee: Go, and remember the captivity of thy fathers in the land of Helam, and in the land of Nephi; and remember how great things he has done for them; for they were in bondage, and he has delivered them. And now I say unto thee, Alma, go thy way, and seek to destroy the church no more, that their prayers may be answered, and this even if thou wilt of thyself be cast off.

27:17 And now it came to pass that these were the last words which the <u>angel</u> spake unto Alma, and he departed.

27:18 And now Alma and those that were with him fell again to the earth, for great was their astonishment; for with their own eyes they had beheld an <u>angel of the Lord</u>; and his voice was as thunder, which shook the earth; and they knew that there was nothing save the power of God that could shake the earth and cause it to tremble as though it would part asunder.

27:19 And now the astonishment of Alma was so great that he became dumb, that he could not open his mouth; yea, and he became weak, even that he could not move his hands; therefore he was taken by those that were with him, and carried helpless, even until he was laid before his father.

27:20 And they rehearsed unto his father all that had happened unto them; and his father rejoiced, for he knew that it was the power of God.

Mosiah 27:32 - Alma begins to teach the people and those who were with him at the time the angel appeared to them

27:32 And now it came to pass that Alma began from this time forward to teach the people, and those who were with Alma at the time the angel appeared unto them, traveling round about through all the land, publishing to all the people the things which they had heard and seen, and preaching the word of God in much tribulation, being greatly persecuted by those who were unbelievers, being smitten by many of them.

ALMA

Alma 8:14-22 - Angel of the Lord appears to Alma commanding him back to Ammonihah to preach again

8:14 And it came to pass that while he was journeying thither, being weighed down with sorrow, wading through much tribulation and anguish of soul, because of the wickedness of the people who were in the city of Ammonihah, it came to pass while Alma was thus weighed down with sorrow, behold an angel of the Lord appeared unto him, saying:

8:15 Blessed art thou, Alma; therefore, lift up thy head and rejoice, for thou hast great cause to rejoice; for thou hast been faithful in keeping the commandments of God from the time which thou receivedst thy first message from him. Behold, I am he that delivered it unto you.

8:16 And behold, I am sent to command thee that thou return to the city of Ammonihah, and preach again unto the people of the city; yea, preach unto them. Yea, say unto them, except they repent the Lord God will destroy them.

8:17 For behold, they do study at this time that they may destroy the liberty of thy people, (for thus saith the Lord) which is contrary to the statutes, and judgments, and commandments which he has given unto his people.

8:18 Now it came to pass that after Alma had received his message from the angel of the Lord he returned speedily to the land of Ammonihah. And he entered the city by another way, yea, by the way which is on the south of the city of Ammonihah.

8:19 And as he entered the city he was an hungered, and he said to a man: Will ye give to an humble servant of God something to eat?

8:20 And the man said unto him: I am a Nephite, and I know that thou art a holy prophet of God, for thou art the man whom an <u>angel</u> said in a vision: Thou shalt receive. Therefore, go with me into my house and I will impart unto thee of my food; and I know that thou wilt be a blessing unto me and my house.

8:21 And it came to pass that the man received him into his house; and the man was called Amulek; and he brought forth bread and meat and set before Alma.

8:22 And it came to pass that Alma ate bread and was filled; and he blessed Amulek and his house, and he gave thanks unto God.

Alma 9:20-34 - Alma preaching to the people of Ammonihah having conversed with angels

9:20 Yea, after having been such a highly favored people of the Lord; yea, after having been favored above every other nation, kindred, tongue, or people; after having had all things made known unto them, according to their desires, and their faith, and prayers, of that which has been, and which is, and which is to come;

9:21 Having been visited by the Spirit of God; having conversed with <u>angels,</u> and having been spoken unto by the voice of the Lord; and having the spirit of prophecy, and the spirit of revelation, and also many gifts, the gift of speaking with tongues, and the gift of preaching, and the gift of the Holy Ghost, and the gift of translation;

9:22 Yea, and after having been delivered of God out of the land of Jerusalem, by the hand of the Lord; having been saved from famine, and from sickness, and all manner of diseases of every kind; and they having waxed strong in battle, that they might not be destroyed; having been brought out of bondage time after time, and having been kept and preserved until now; and they have been prospered until they are rich in all manner of things –

9:23 And now behold I say unto you, that if this people, who have received so many blessings from the hand of the Lord, should transgress contrary to the light and knowledge which they do have, I say unto you that if this be the case, that if they should fall into transgression, it would be far more tolerable for the Lamanites than for them.

9:24 For behold, the promises of the Lord are extended to the Lamanites, but they are not unto you if ye transgress; for has not the Lord expressly promised and firmly decreed, that if ye will rebel against him that ye shall utterly be destroyed from off the face of the earth?

9:25 And now for this cause, that ye may not be destroyed, the Lord has sent his angel to visit many of his people, declaring unto them that they must go forth and cry mightily unto this people, saying: Repent ye, for the kingdom of heaven is nigh at hand;

9:26 And not many days hence the Son of God shall come in his glory; and his glory shall be the glory of the Only Begotten of the Father, full of grace, equity, and truth, full of patience, mercy, and long-suffering, quick to hear the cries of his people and to answer their prayers.

9:27 And behold, he cometh to redeem those who will be baptized unto repentance, through faith on his name.

9:28 Therefore, prepare ye the way of the Lord, for the time is at hand that all men shall reap a reward of their works, according to that which they have been – if they have been righteous they shall reap the salvation of their souls, according to the power and deliverance of Jesus Christ; and if they have been evil they shall reap the damnation of their souls, according to the power and captivation of the devil.

9:29 Now behold, this is the voice of the angel, crying unto the people.

9:30 And now, my beloved brethren, for ye are my brethren, and ye ought to be beloved, and ye ought to bring forth works which are meet for repentance, seeing that your hearts have been grossly hardened against the word of God, and seeing that ye are a lost and a fallen people.

9:31 Now it came to pass that when I, Alma, had spoken these words, behold, the people were wroth with me because I said unto them that they were a hard-hearted and a stiffnecked people.

9:32 And also because I said unto them that they were a lost and a fallen people they were angry with me, and sought to lay their hands upon me, that they might cast me into prison.

9:33 But it came to pass that the Lord did not suffer them that they should take me at that time and cast me into prison.

9:34 And it came to pass that Amulek went and stood forth, and began to preach unto them also. And now the words of Amulek are not all written, nevertheless a part of his words are written in this book.

Alma 10:6-11 - Amulek speaks about the angel of the Lord appearing to him and caring for the holy man Alma

10:6 Nevertheless, I did harden my heart, for I was called many times and I would not hear; therefore I knew concerning these things, yet I would not know; therefore I went on rebelling against God, in the wickedness of my heart, even until the fourth day of this seventh month, which is in the tenth year of the reign of the judges.

10:7 As I was journeying to see a very near kindred, behold an angel of the Lord appeared unto me and said: Amulek, return to thine own house, for thou shalt feed a prophet of the Lord; yea, a holy man, who is a chosen man of God; for he has fasted many days because of the sins of this people, and he is an hungered, and thou shalt receive him into thy house and feed him, and he shall bless thee and thy house; and the blessing of the Lord shall rest upon thee and thy house.

10:8 And it came to pass that I obeyed the voice of the angel, and returned towards my house. And as I was going thither I found the man whom the angel said unto me: Thou shalt receive into thy house – and behold it was this same man who has been speaking unto you concerning the things of God.

10:9 And the <u>angel</u> said unto me he is a holy man; wherefore I know he is a holy man because it was said by an <u>angel of God</u>.

10:10 And again, I know that the things whereof he hath testified are true; for behold I say unto you, that as the Lord liveth, even so has he sent his <u>angel</u> to make these things manifest unto me; and this he has done while this Alma hath dwelt at my house.

10:11 For behold, he hath blessed mine house, he hath blessed me, and my women, and my children, and my father and my kinsfolk; yea, even all my kindred hath he blessed, and the blessing of the Lord hath rested upon us according to the words which he spake.

Alma 10:20-21 - The voice of God's angels cry unto the people of Ammonihah to repent

10:20 And now I say unto you that well doth the Lord judge of your iniquities; well doth he cry unto this people, by the voice of his <u>angels</u>: Repent ye, repent, for the kingdom of heaven is at hand.

10:21 Yea, well doth he cry, by the voice of his <u>angels</u> that: I will come down among my people, with equity and justice in my hands.

Alma 11:1-31 - Zeezrom asks Amulek how he knows these things, and Amulek says an angel hath made them known to me

11:1 Now it was in the law of Mosiah that every man who was a judge of the law, or those who were appointed to be judges, should receive wages according to the time which they labored to judge those who were brought before them to be judged.

11:2 Now if a man owed another, and he would not pay that which he did owe, he was complained of to the judge; and the judge executed authority, and sent forth officers that the man should be brought before him; and he judged the man according to the law and the evidences which were brought against him, and thus the man was compelled to pay that which he owed, or be stripped, or be cast out from among the people as a thief and a robber.

11:3 And the judge received for his wages according to his time – a senine of gold for a day, or a senum of silver, which is equal to a senine of gold; and this is according to the law which was given.

11:4 Now these are the names of the different pieces of their gold, and of their silver, according to their value. And the names are given by the Nephites, for they did not reckon after the manner of the Jews who were at Jerusalem; neither did they measure after the manner of the Jews; but they altered their reckoning and their measure, according to the minds and the circumstances of the people, in every generation, until the reign of the judges, they having been established by king Mosiah.

11:5 Now the reckoning is thus – a senine of gold, a seon of gold, a shum of gold, and a limnah of gold.

11:6 A senum of silver, an amnor of silver, an ezrom of silver, and an onti of silver.

11:7 A senum of silver was equal to a senine of gold, and either for a measure of barley, and also for a measure of every kind of grain.

11:8 Now the amount of a seon of gold was twice the value of a senine.

11:9 And a shum of gold was twice the value of a seon.

11:10 And a limnah of gold was the value of them all.

11:11 And an amnor of silver was as great as two senums.

11:12 And an ezrom of silver was as great as four senums.

11:13 And an onti was as great as them all.

11:14 Now this is the value of the lesser numbers of their reckoning –

11:15 A shiblon is half of a senum; therefore, a shiblon for half a measure of barley.

11:16 And a shiblum is a half of a shiblon.

11:17 And a leah is the half of a shiblum.

11:18 Now this is their number, according to their reckoning.

11:19 Now an antion of gold is equal to three shiblons.

11:20 Now, it was for the sole purpose to get gain, because they received their wages according to their employ, therefore, they did stir up the people to riotings, and all manner of disturbances and wickedness, that they might have more employ, that they might get money according to the suits which were brought before them; therefore they did stir up the people against Alma and Amulek.

11:21 And this Zeezrom began to question Amulek, saying: Will ye answer me a few questions which I shall ask you? Now Zeezrom was a man who was expert in the devices of the devil, that he might destroy that which was good; therefore, he said unto Amulek: Will ye answer the questions which I shall put unto you?

11:22 And Amulek said unto him: Yea, if it be according to the Spirit of the Lord, which is in me; for I shall say nothing which is contrary to the Spirit of the Lord. And Zeezrom said unto him: Behold, here are six onties of silver, and all these will I give thee if thou wilt deny the existence of a Supreme Being.

11:23 Now Amulek said: O thou child of hell, why tempt ye me? Knowest thou that the righteous yieldeth to no such temptations?

11:24 Believest thou that there is no God? I say unto you, Nay, thou knowest that there is a God, but thou lovest that lucre more than him.

11:25 And now thou hast lied before God unto me. Thou saidst unto me – Behold these six onties, which are of great worth, I will give unto thee – when thou hadst it in thy heart to retain them from me; and it was only thy desire that I should deny the true and living God, that thou mightest have cause to destroy me. And now behold, for this great evil thou shalt have thy reward.

11:26 And Zeezrom said unto him: Thou sayest there is a true and living God?

11:27 And Amulek said: Yea, there is a true and living God.

11:28 Now Zeezrom said: Is there more than one God?

11:29 And he answered, No.

11:30 Now Zeezrom said unto him again: How knowest thou these things?

11:31 And he said: An <u>angel</u> hath made them known unto me.

Alma 12:20-30 - Cherubim and a flaming sword on the east gate of the garden of Eden and God sent angels to converse with men and made known the plan of redemption

12:20 But there was one Antionah, who was a chief ruler among them, came forth and said unto him: What is this that thou hast said, that man should rise from the dead and be changed from this mortal to an immortal state that the soul can never die?

12:21 What does the scripture mean, which saith that God placed <u>cherubim</u> and a flaming sword on the east of the garden of Eden, lest our first parents should enter and partake of the fruit of the tree of life, and live forever? And thus we see that there was no possible chance that they should live forever.

12:22 Now Alma said unto him: This is the thing which I was about to explain, now we see that Adam did fall by the partaking of the forbidden fruit, according to the word of God; and thus we see, that by his fall, all mankind became a lost and fallen people.

12:23 And now behold, I say unto you that if it had been possible for Adam to have partaken of the fruit of the tree of life at that time, there would have been no death, and the word would have been void, making God a liar, for he said: If thou eat thou shalt surely die.

12:24 And we see that death comes upon mankind, yea, the death which has been spoken of by Amulek, which is the temporal death; nevertheless there was a space granted unto man in which he might repent; therefore this life became a probationary state; a time to prepare to meet God; a time to prepare for that endless state which has been spoken of by us, which is after the resurrection of the dead.

12:25 Now, if it had not been for the plan of redemption, which was laid from the foundation of the world, there could have been no resurrection of the dead; but there was a plan of redemption laid, which shall bring to pass the resurrection of the dead, of which has been spoken.

12:26 And now behold, if it were possible that our first parents could have gone forth and partaken of the tree of life they would have been forever miserable, having no preparatory state; and thus the plan of redemption would have been frustrated, and the word of God would have been void, taking none effect.

12:27 But behold, it was not so; but it was appointed unto men that they must die; and after death, they must come to judgment, even that same judgment of which we have spoken, which is the end.

12:28 And after God had appointed that these things should come unto man, behold, then he saw that it was expedient that man should know concerning the things whereof he had appointed unto them;

12:29 Therefore he sent <u>angels</u> to converse with them, who caused men to behold of his glory.

12:30 And they began from that time forth to call on his name; therefore God conversed with men, and made known unto them the plan of redemption, which had been prepared from the foundation of the world; and this he made known unto them according to their faith and repentance and their holy works.

Alma 13:21-26 - Alma speaks about the voice of the Lord by mouth of angels declaring glad tidings

13:21 And now it came to pass that when Alma had said these words unto them, he stretched forth his hand unto them and cried with a mighty voice, saying: Now is the time to repent, for the day of salvation draweth nigh;

13:22 Yea, and the voice of the Lord, by the mouth of <u>angels</u>, doth declare it unto all nations; yea, doth declare it, that they may have glad tidings of great joy; yea, and he doth sound these glad tidings among all his people, yea, even to them that are scattered abroad upon the face of the earth; wherefore they have come unto us.

13:23 And they are made known unto us in plain terms, that we may understand, that we cannot err; and this because of our being wanderers in a strange land; therefore, we are thus highly favored, for we have these glad tidings declared unto us in all parts of our vineyard.

13:24 For behold, <u>angels</u> are declaring it unto many at this time in our land; and this is for the purpose of preparing the hearts of the children of men to receive his word at the time of his coming in his glory.

13:25 And now we only wait to hear the joyful news declared unto us by the mouth of angels, of his coming; for the time cometh, we know not how soon. Would to God that it might be in my day; but let it be sooner or later, in it I will rejoice.

13:26 And it shall be made known unto just and holy men, by the mouth of <u>angels,</u> at the time of his coming, that the words of our fathers may be fulfilled, according to that which they have spoken concerning him, which was according to the spirit of prophecy which was in them.

Alma 17:2 - Sons of Mosiah were with Alma at the time the angel first appeared unto him

17:2 Now these sons of Mosiah were with Alma at the time the <u>angel</u> first appeared unto him; therefore Alma did rejoice exceedingly to see his brethren; and what added more to his joy, they were still his brethren in the Lord; yea, and they had waxed strong in the knowledge of the truth; for they were men of a sound understanding and they had searched the scriptures diligently, that they might know the word of God.

Alma 18:30-32 - Ammon teaches king Lamoni about heavens where God dwells and all his holy angels

18:30 And Ammon said unto him: The heavens is a place where God dwells and all his holy <u>angels</u>.

18:31 And king Lamoni said: Is it above the earth?

18:32 And Ammon said: Yea, and he looketh down upon all the children of men; and he knows all the thoughts and intents of the heart; for by his hand were they all created from the beginning.

Alma 19:33-36 - Ammon ministered to people and servants of Lamoni and the people declared that they had seen angels and conversed with them

19:33 And it came to pass that when Ammon arose he also administered unto them, and also did all the servants of Lamoni; and they did all declare unto the people the selfsame thing – that their hearts had been changed; that they had no more desire to do evil.

19:34 And behold, many did declare unto the people that they had seen angels and had conversed with them; and thus they had told them things of God, and of his righteousness.

19:35 And it came to pass that there were many that did believe in their words; and as many as did believe were baptized; and they became a righteous people, and they did establish a church among them.

19:36 And thus the work of the Lord did commence among the Lamanites; thus the Lord did begin to pour out his Spirit upon them; and we see that his arm is extended to all people who will repent and believe on his name.

Alma 21:5 - As Aarom is speaking in a synagogue, an Amalekite contends with him about seeing angels and why angels do not appear to them

21:5 Therefore, as Aaron entered into one of their synagogues to preach unto the people, and as he was speaking unto them, behold there arose an Amalekite and began to contend with him, saying: What is that thou hast testified? Hast thou seen an angel? Why do not angels appear unto us? Behold are not this people as good as thy people?

Alma 24:14 - God visits the Anti-Nephi-Lehies by his angels, that the plan of salvation be made known to them

24:14 And the great God has had mercy on us, and made these things known unto us that we might not perish; yea, and he has made these things known unto us beforehand, because he loveth our souls as well as he loveth our children; therefore, in his mercy he doth visit us by his <u>angels</u>, that the plan of salvation might be made known unto us as well as unto future generations.

Alma 27:3-5 - Ammon and brethren treated like angels sent from God to save the people of Anti-Nephi-Lehi from everlasting destruction

27:3 Now this people again refused to take their arms, and they suffered themselves to be slain according to the desires of their enemies.

27:4 Now when Ammon and his brethren saw this work of destruction among those whom they so dearly beloved, and among those who had so dearly beloved them – for they were treated as though they were <u>angels</u> sent from God to save them from everlasting destruction – therefore, when Ammon and his brethren saw this great work of destruction, they were moved with compassion, and they said unto the king:

27:5 Let us gather together this people of the Lord, and let us go down to the land of Zarahemla to our brethren the Nephites, and flee out of the hands of our enemies, that we be not destroyed.

Alma 29:1-9 - Alma wishes to be an angel and to go forth and speak with the trump of God and voice to shake the earth and cry repentance and speak unto all the ends of the earth

29:1 O that I were an <u>angel,</u> and could have the wish of mine heart, that I might go forth and speak with the trump of God, with a voice to shake the earth, and cry repentance unto every people!

29:2 Yea, I would declare unto every soul, as with the voice of thunder, repentance and the plan of redemption, that they should repent and come unto our God, that there might not be more sorrow upon all the face of the earth.

29:3 But behold, I am a man, and do sin in my wish; for I ought to be content with the things which the Lord hath allotted unto me.

29:4 I ought not to harrow up in my desires, the firm decree of a just God, for I know that he granteth unto men according to their desire, whether it be unto death or unto life; yea, I know that he allotteth unto men, yea, decreeth unto them decrees which are unalterable, according to their wills, whether they be unto salvation or unto destruction.

29:5 Yea, and I know that good and evil have come before all men; he that knoweth not good from evil is blameless; but he that knoweth good and evil, to him it is given according to his desires, whether he desireth good or evil, life or death, joy or remorse of conscience.

29:6 Now, seeing that I know these things, why should I desire more than to perform the work to which I have been called?

29:7 Why should I desire that I were an <u>angel,</u> that I could speak unto all the ends of the earth?

29:8 For behold, the Lord doth grant unto all nations, of their own nation and tongue, to teach his word, yea, in wisdom, all that he seeth fit that they should have; therefore we see that the Lord doth counsel in wisdom, according to that which is just and true.

29:9 I know that which the Lord hath commanded me, and I glory in it. I do not glory of myself, but I glory in that which the Lord hath commanded me; yea, and this is my glory, that perhaps I may be an instrument in the hands of God to bring some soul to repentance; and this is my joy.

Alma 30:52-56 - The devil had appeared to Korihor in the form of an angel and taught him what to say

30:52 And Korihor put forth his hand and wrote, saying: I know that I am dumb, for I cannot speak; and I know that nothing save it were the power of God could bring this upon me; yea, and I always knew that there was a God.

30:53 But behold, the devil hath deceived me; for he appeared unto me in the form of an angel, and said unto me: Go and reclaim this people, for they have all gone astray after an unknown God. And he said unto me: There is no God; yea, and he taught me that which I should say. And I have taught his words; and I taught them because they were pleasing unto the carnal mind; and I taught them, even until I had much success, insomuch that I verily believed that they were true; and for this cause I withstood the truth, even until I have brought this great curse upon me.

30:54 Now when he had said this, he besought that Alma should pray unto God, that the curse might be taken from him.

30:55 But Alma said unto him: If this curse should be taken from thee thou wouldst again lead away the hearts of this people; therefore, it shall be unto thee even as the Lord will.

30:56 And it came to pass that the curse was not taken off of Korihor; but he was cast out, and went about from house to house begging for his food.

Alma 32:21-25 - Alma teaches that God imparts his word by angels unto men, women and children

32:21 And now as I said concerning faith – faith is not to have a perfect knowledge of things; therefore if ye have faith ye hope for things which are not seen, which are true.

32:22 And now, behold, I say unto you, and I would that ye should remember, that God is merciful unto all who believe on his name; therefore he desireth, in the first place, that ye should believe, yea, even on his word.

32:23 And now, he imparteth his word by <u>angels</u> unto men, yea, not only men but women also. Now this is not all; little children do have words given unto them many times which confound the wise and the learned.

32:24 And now, my beloved brethren, as ye have desired to know of me what ye shall do because ye are afflicted and cast out – now I do not desire that ye should suppose that I mean to judge you only according to that which is true –

32:25 For I do not mean that ye all of you have been compelled to humble yourselves; for I verily believe that there are some among you who would humble themselves, let them be in whatsoever circumstances they might.

Alma 36:3-11 - Alma telling son Helaman those things told and happened to him by God's holy angel

36:3 And now, O my son Helaman, behold, thou art in thy youth, and therefore, I beseech of thee that thou wilt hear my words and learn of me; for I do know that whosoever shall put their trust in God shall be supported in their trials, and their troubles, and their afflictions, and shall be lifted up at the last day.

36:4 And I would not that ye think that I know of myself – not of the temporal but of the spiritual, not of the carnal mind but of God.

36:5 Now, behold, I say unto you, if I had not been born of God I should not have known these things; but God has, by the mouth of his holy <u>angel</u>, made these things known unto me, not of any worthiness of myself.

36:6 For I went about with the sons of Mosiah, seeking to destroy the church of God; but behold, God sent his holy <u>angel</u> to stop us by the way.

36:7 And behold, he spake unto us, as it were the voice of thunder, and the whole earth did tremble beneath our feet; and we all fell to the earth, for the fear of the Lord came upon us.

36:8 But behold, the voice said unto me: Arise. And I arose and stood up, and beheld the <u>angel</u>.

36:9 And he said unto me: If thou wilt of thyself be destroyed, seek no more to destroy the church of God.

36:10 And it came to pass that I fell to the earth; and it was for the space of three days and three nights that I could not open my mouth, neither had I the use of my limbs.

36:11 And the <u>angel</u> spake more things unto me, which were heard by my brethren, but I did not hear them; for when I heard the words – If thou wilt be destroyed of thyself, seek no more to destroy the church of God – I was struck with such great fear and amazement lest perhaps I should be destroyed, that I fell to the earth and I did hear no more.

Alma 36:21-23 - Alma sees the vision his father Lehi saw, God sitting on his throne surrounded by numberless concourses of angels

36:21 Yea, I say unto you, my son, that there could be nothing so exquisite and so bitter as were my pains. Yea, and again I say unto you, my son, that on the other hand, there can be nothing so exquisite and sweet as was my joy.

36:22 Yea, methought I saw, even as our father Lehi saw, God sitting upon his throne, surrounded with numberless concourses of <u>angels</u>, in the attitude of singing and praising their God; yea, and my soul did long to be there.

36:23 But behold, my limbs did receive their strength again, and I stood upon my feet, and did manifest unto the people that I had been born of God.

Alma 38:5-9 - Alma testifies to son Shiblon about visitation of an angel declaring that he must stop the work of destruction among his people

38:5 And now my son, Shiblon, I would that ye should remember, that as much as ye shall put your trust in God even so much ye shall be delivered out of your trials, and your troubles, and your afflictions, and ye shall be lifted up at the last day.

38:6 Now, my son, I would not that ye should think that I know these things of myself, but it is the Spirit of God which is in me which maketh these things known unto me; for if I had not been born of God I should not have known these things.

38:7 But behold, the Lord in his great mercy sent his <u>angel</u> to declare unto me that I must stop the work of destruction among his people; yea, and I have seen an <u>angel</u> face to face, and he spake with me, and his voice was as thunder, and it shook the whole earth.

38:8 And it came to pass that I was three days and three nights in the most bitter pain and anguish of soul; and never, until I did cry out unto the Lord Jesus Christ for mercy, did I receive a remission of my sins. But behold, I did cry unto him and I did find peace to my soul.

38:9 And now, my son, I have told you this that ye may learn wisdom, that ye may learn of me that there is no other way or means whereby man can be saved, only in and through Christ. Behold, he is the life and the light of the world. Behold, he is the word of truth and righteousness.

Alma 39:16-19 - Alma tells son is it not just as easy for the Lord to send his angel to declare these glad tidings after his coming?

39:16 And now, my son, this was the ministry unto which ye were called, to declare these glad tidings unto this people to prepare their minds; or rather that salvation might come unto them, that they may prepare the minds of their children to hear the word at the time of his coming.

39:17 And now I will ease your mind somewhat on this subject. Behold, you marvel why these things should be known so long beforehand. Behold, I say unto you, is not a soul at this time as precious unto God as a soul will be at the time of his coming?

39:18 Is it not as necessary that the plan of redemption should be made known unto this people as well as unto their children?

39:19 Is it not as easy at this time for the Lord to send his <u>angel</u> to declare these glad tidings unto us as unto our children, or as after the time of his coming?

Alma 40:11-14 - Angel told Alma about what happens to the spirits of all departed men, the righteous and the evil

40:11 Now, concerning the state of the soul between death and the resurrection – Behold, it has been made known unto me by an <u>angel,</u> that the spirits of all men, as soon as they are departed from this mortal body, yea, the spirits of all men, whether they be good or evil, are taken home to that God who gave them life.

40:12 And then shall it come to pass, that the spirits of those who are righteous are received into a state of happiness, which is called paradise, a state of rest, a state of peace, where they shall rest from all their troubles and from all care, and sorrow.

40:13 And then shall it come to pass, that the spirits of the wicked, yea, who are evil – for behold, they have no part nor portion of the Spirit of the Lord; for behold, they chose evil works rather than good; therefore the spirit of the devil did enter into them, and take possession of their house – and these shall be cast out into outer darkness; there shall be weeping, and wailing, and gnashing of teeth, and this because of their own iniquity, being led captive by the will of the devil.

40:14 Now this is the state of the souls of the wicked, yea, in darkness, and a state of awful, fearful looking for the fiery indignation of the wrath of God upon them; thus they remain in this state, as well as the righteous in paradise, until the time of their resurrection.

Alma 42:2-4 - Alma tells son about the Cherubim and the flaming sword to keep the tree of life from man that he should not partake of the fruit

42:2 Now behold, my son, I will explain this thing unto thee. For behold, after the Lord God sent our first parents forth from the garden of Eden, to till the ground, from whence they were taken – yea, he drew out the man, and he placed at the east end of the garden of Eden, cherubim, and a flaming sword which turned every way, to keep the tree of life -

42:3 Now, we see that the man had become as God, knowing good and evil; and lest he should put forth his hand, and take also of the tree of life, and eat and live forever, the Lord God placed cherubim and the flaming sword, that he should not partake of the fruit -

42:4 And thus we see, that there was a time granted unto man to repent, yea, a probationary time, a time to repent and serve God.

HELAMAN

Helaman 5:11 - Nephi and Lehi rmember the words of Amulek to Zeezrom about the Father who sent his angels to declare the tidings of the conditions of repentance

5:11 And he hath power given unto him from the Father to redeem them from their sins because of repentance; therefore he hath sent his angels to declare the tidings of the conditions of repentance, which bringeth unto the power of the Redeemer, unto the salvation of their souls.

Helaman 5:36-41 - Aminadab said unto the Lamanites that angels of God conversed with Nephi and Lehi and their faces shine exceedingly, even as the faces of angels

5:36 And it came to pass that he turned him about, and behold, he saw through the cloud of darkness the faces of Nephi and Lehi; and behold, they did shine exceedingly, even as the faces of <u>angels</u>. And he beheld that they did lift their eyes to heaven; and they were in the attitude as if talking or lifting their voices to some being whom they beheld.

5:37 And it came to pass that this man did cry unto the multitude, that they might turn and look. And behold, there was power given unto them that they did turn and look; and they did behold the faces of Nephi and Lehi.

5:38 And they said unto the man: Behold, what do all these things mean, and who is it with whom these men do converse?

5:39 Now the man's name was Aminadab. And Aminadab said unto them: They do converse with the <u>angels of God</u>.

5:40 And it came to pass that the Lamanites said unto him: What shall we do, that this cloud of darkness may be removed from overshadowing us?

5:41 And Aminadab said unto them: You must repent, and cry unto the voice, even until ye shall have faith in Christ, who was taught unto you by Alma, and Amulek, and Zeezrom; and when ye shall do this, the cloud of darkness shall be removed from overshadowing you.

Helaman 5:46-49 - Heavens opened and angels came down and ministered unto Nephi and Lehi

5:46 And it came to pass that there came a voice unto them, yea, a pleasant voice, as if it were a whisper, saying:

5:47 Peace, peace be unto you, because of your faith in my Well Beloved, who was from the foundation of the world.

5:48 And now, when they heard this they cast up their eyes as if to behold from whence the voice came; and behold, they saw the heavens open; and <u>angels</u> came down out of heaven and ministered unto them.

5:49 And there were about three hundred souls who saw and heard these things; and they were bidden to go forth and marvel not, neither should they doubt.

Helaman 10:6-7 - God gives Nephi power over this people in the presence of the angels

10:6 Behold, thou art Nephi, and I am God. Behold, I declare it unto thee in the presence of mine <u>angels</u>, that ye shall have power over this people, and shall smite the earth with famine, and with pestilence, and destruction, according to the wickedness of this people.

10:7 Behold, I give unto you power, that whatsoever ye shall seal on earth shall be sealed in heaven; and whatsoever ye shall loose on earth shall be loosed in heaven; and thus shall ye have power among this people.

Helaman 13:7 - Samuel the Lamanite prophesies to the Nephites about what an angel of the Lord declared to him

13:7 And behold, an <u>angel of the Lord</u> hath declared it unto me, and he did bring glad tidings to my soul. And behold, I was sent unto you to declare it unto you also, that ye might have glad tidings; but behold ye would not receive me.

Helaman 13:37 - Samuel the Laminite prophesies to the Nephites about being surrounded by demons and encircled by the angels of him who hath sought to destroy our souls

13:37 Behold, we are surrounded by demons, yea, we are encircled about by the <u>angels</u> of him who hath sought to destroy our souls. Behold, our iniquities are great. O Lord, canst thou not turn away thine anger from us? And this shall be your language in those days.

Helaman 14:9 - Samuel prophesies as commanded by an angel of the Lord, to repent and prepare the way of the Lord

14:9 And behold, thus hath the Lord commanded me, by his <u>angel</u>, that I should come and tell this thing unto you; yea, he hath commanded that I should prophesy these things unto you; yea, he hath said unto me: Cry unto this people, repent and prepare the way of the Lord.

Helaman 14:26-29 - Samuel prophesies what the angel spoke to him about the time of judgment

14:26 And behold, thus hath the <u>angel</u> spoken unto me; for he said unto me that there should be thunderings and lightnings for the space of many hours.

14:27 And he said unto me that while the thunder and the lightning lasted, and the tempest, that these things should be, and that darkness should cover the face of the whole earth for the space of three days.

14:28 And the <u>angel</u> said unto me that many shall see greater things than these, to the intent that they might believe that these signs and these wonders should come to pass upon all the face of this land, to the intent that there should be no cause for unbelief among the children of men –

14:29 And this to the intent that whosoever will believe might be saved, and that whosoever will not believe, a righteous judgment might come upon them; and also if they are condemned they bring upon themselves their own condemnation.

Helaman 16:13-14 - Angels appearing to men and wise men and declared glad tiding of great joy thus in this year the scriptures began to be fulfilled

16:13 But it came to pass in the ninetieth year of the reign of the judges, there were great signs given unto the people, and wonders; and the words of the prophets began to be fulfilled.

16:14 And angels did appear unto men, wise men, and did declare unto them glad tidings of great joy; thus in this year the scriptures began to be fulfilled.

3 NEPHI

3 Nephi 7:15-18 - Angels visit Nephi and having seen angels, had power given unto him, that he might know concerning the ministry of Christ

7:15 And it came to pass that Nephi – having been visited by angels and also the voice of the Lord, therefore having seen angels, and being eye-witness, and having had power given unto him that he might know concerning the ministry of Christ, and also being eye-witness to their quick return from righteousness unto their wickedness and abominations;

7:16 Therefore, being grieved for the hardness of their hearts and the blindness of their minds – went forth among them in that same year, and began to testify, boldly, repentance and remission of sins through faith on the Lord Jesus Christ.

7:17 And he did minister many things unto them; and all of them cannot be written, and a part of them would not suffice, therefore they are not written in this book. And Nephi did minister with power and with great authority.

7:18 And it came to pass that they were angry with him, even because he had greater power than they, for it were not possible that they could disbelieve his words, for so great was his faith on the Lord Jesus Christ that <u>angels</u> did minister unto him daily.

3 Nephi 9:1-2 - A voice cried out about the devil who laugheth, and his angels rejoice

9:1 And it came to pass that there was a voice heard among all the inhabitants of the earth, upon all the face of this land, crying:

9:2 Wo, wo, wo unto this people; wo unto the inhabitants of the whole earth except they shall repent; for the devil laugheth, and his <u>angels</u> rejoice, because of the slain of the fair sons and daughters of my people; and it is because of their iniquity and abominations that they are fallen!

3 Nephi 11:8 - Christ appears to the people of Nephi and they thought he was an angel

11:8 And it came to pass, as they understood they cast their eyes up again towards heaven; and behold, they saw a Man descending out of heaven; and he was clothed in a white robe; and he came down and stood in the midst of them; and the eyes of the whole multitude were turned upon him, and they durst not open their mouths, even one to another, and wist not what it meant, for they thought it was an <u>angel</u> that had appeared unto them.

3 Nephi 17:23-25 - Jesus speaks about the children and they look up to the heavens which open and angels descending out of heaven encircled them and did minister unto them

17:23 And he spake unto the multitude, and said unto them: Behold your little ones.

17:24 And as they looked to behold they cast their eyes towards heaven, and they saw the heavens open, and they saw <u>angels</u> descending out of heaven as it were in the midst of fire; and they came down and encircled those little ones about, and they were encircled about with fire; and the <u>angels</u> did minister unto them.

17:25 And the multitude did see and hear and bear record; and they know that their record is true for they all of them did see and hear, every man for himself; and they were in number about two thousand and five hundred souls; and they did consist of men, women, and children.

3 Nephi 19:11-15 - Nephi baptized all those whom Jesus had chosen and the Holy Ghost did fall upon them and angels came down from heaven and ministered unto them and unto the disciples

19:11 And it came to pass that Nephi went down into the water and was baptized.

19:12 And he came up out of the water and began to baptize. And he baptized all those whom Jesus had chosen.

19:13 And it came to pass when they were all baptized and had come up out of the water, the Holy Ghost did fall upon them, and they were filled with the Holy Ghost and with fire.

19:14 And behold, they were encircled about as if it were by fire; and it came down from heaven, and the multitude did witness it, and did bear record; and <u>angels</u> did come down out of heaven and did minister unto them.

19:15 And it came to pass that while the <u>angels</u> were ministering unto the disciples, behold, Jesus came and stood in the midst and ministered unto them.

3 Nephi 27:30 - Jesus' joy is great and rejoices with the Father and all the holy angels

27:30 And now, behold, my joy is great, even unto fulness, because of you, and also this generation; yea, and even the Father rejoiceth, and also all the holy <u>angels,</u> because of you and this generation; for none of them are lost.

3 Nephi 28:24-30 - Mormon speaks about those who were never to taste death and they are as the angels of God

28:24 And now I, Mormon, make an end of speaking concerning these things for a time.

28:25 Behold, I was about to write the names of those who were never to taste of death, but the Lord forbade; therefore I write them not, for they are hid from the world.

28:26 But behold, I have seen them, and they have ministered unto me.

28:27 And behold they will be among the Gentiles, and the Gentiles shall know them not.

28:28 They will also be among the Jews, and the Jews shall know them not.

28:29 And it shall come to pass, when the Lord seeth fit in his wisdom that they shall minister unto all the scattered tribes of Israel, and unto all nations, kindreds, tongues and people, and shall bring out of them unto Jesus many souls, that their desire may be fulfilled, and also because of the convincing power of God which is in them.

28:30 And they are as the <u>angels of God,</u> and if they shall pray unto the Father in the name of Jesus they can show themselves unto whatsoever man it seemeth them good.

MORONI

Moroni 7:17 - Mormon speaks about the devil work and his angels

7:17 But whatsoever thing persuadeth men to do evil, and believe not in Christ, and deny him, and serve not God, then ye may know with a perfect knowledge it is of the devil; for after this manner doth the devil work, for he persuadeth no man to do good, no, not one; neither do his <u>angels</u>; neither do they who subject themselves unto him.

Moroni 7:22-48 - Mormon speaks about God sending angels to minister unto the children of men and to make manifest the coming of Christ - By the ministering of angels, men begin to exercise faith in Christ - Miracles have not ceased, neither have angels ceased to minister unto the children of men - Have angels ceased to appear unto the children of men? Nay, and it is by faith that angels appear and minister unto men

7:22 For behold, God knowing all things, being from everlasting to everlasting, behold, he sent <u>angels</u> to minister unto the children of men, to make manifest concerning the coming of Christ; and in Christ there should come every good thing.

7:23 And God also declared unto prophets, by his own mouth, that Christ should come.

7:24 And behold, there were divers ways that he did manifest things unto the children of men, which were good; and all things which are good cometh of Christ; otherwise men were fallen, and there could no good thing come unto them.

7:25 Wherefore, by the ministering of <u>angels</u>, and by every word which proceeded forth out of the mouth of God, men began to exercise faith in Christ; and thus by faith, they did lay hold upon every good thing; and thus it was until the coming of Christ.

7:26 And after that he came men also were saved by faith in his name; and by faith, they become the sons of God. And as sure as Christ liveth he spake these words unto our fathers, saying: Whatsoever thing ye shall ask the Father in my name, which is good, in faith believing that ye shall receive, behold, it shall be done unto you.

7:27 Wherefore, my beloved brethren, have miracles ceased because Christ hath ascended into heaven, and hath sat down on the right hand of God, to claim of the Father his rights of mercy which he hath upon the children of men?

7:28 For he hath answered the ends of the law, and he claimeth all those who have faith in him; and they who have faith in him will cleave unto every good thing; wherefore he advocateth the cause of the children of men; and he dwelleth eternally in the heavens.

7:29 And because he hath done this, my beloved brethren, have miracles ceased? Behold I say unto you, Nay; neither have <u>angels</u> ceased to minister unto the children of men.

7:30 For behold, they are subject unto him, to minister according to the word of his command, showing themselves unto them of strong faith and a firm mind in every form of godliness.

7:31 And the office of their ministry is to call men unto repentance, and to fulfill and to do the work of the covenants of the Father, which he hath made unto the children of men, to prepare the way among the children of men, by declaring the word of Christ unto the chosen vessels of the Lord, that they may bear testimony of him.

7:32 And by so doing, the Lord God prepareth the way that the residue of men may have faith in Christ, that the Holy Ghost may have place in their hearts, according to the power thereof; and after this manner bringeth to pass the Father, the covenants which he hath made unto the children of men.

7:33 And Christ hath said: If ye will have faith in me ye shall have power to do whatsoever thing is expedient in me.

7:34 And he hath said: Repent all ye ends of the earth, and come unto me, and be baptized in my name, and have faith in me, that ye may be saved.

7:35 And now, my beloved brethren, if this be the case that these things are true which I have spoken unto you, and God will show unto you, with power and great glory at the last day, that they are true, and if they are true has the day of miracles ceased?

7:36 Or have <u>angels</u> ceased to appear unto the children of men? Or has he withheld the power of the Holy Ghost from them? Or will he, so long as time shall last, or the earth shall stand, or there shall be one man upon the face thereof to be saved?

7:37 Behold I say unto you, Nay; for it is by faith that miracles are wrought; and it is by faith that <u>angels</u> appear and minister unto men; wherefore, if these things have ceased wo be unto the children of men, for it is because of unbelief, and all is vain.

7:38 For no man can be saved, according to the words of Christ, save they shall have faith in his name; wherefore, if these things have ceased, then has faith ceased also; and awful is the state of man, for they are as though there had been no redemption made.

7:39 But behold, my beloved brethren, I judge better things of you, for I judge that ye have faith in Christ because of your meekness; for if ye have not faith in him then ye are not fit to be numbered among the people of his church.

7:40 And again, my beloved brethren, I would speak unto you concerning hope. How is it that ye can attain unto faith, save ye shall have hope?

7:41 And what is it that ye shall hope for? Behold I say unto you that ye shall have hope through the atonement of Christ and the power of his resurrection, to be raised unto life eternal, and this because of your faith in him according to the promise.

7:42 Wherefore, if a man have faith he must needs have hope; for without faith there cannot be any hope.

7:43 And again, behold I say unto you that he cannot have faith and hope, save he shall be meek, and lowly of heart.

7:44 If so, his faith and hope is vain, for none is acceptable before God, save the meek and lowly in heart; and if a man be meek and lowly in heart, and confesses by the power of the Holy Ghost that Jesus is the Christ, he must needs have charity; for if he have not charity he is nothing; wherefore he must needs have charity.

7:45 And charity suffereth long, and is kind, and envieth not, and is not puffed up, seeketh not her own, is not easily provoked, thinketh no evil, and rejoiceth not in iniquity but rejoiceth in the truth, beareth all things, believeth all things, hopeth all things, endureth all things.

7:46 Wherefore, my beloved brethren, if ye have not charity, ye are nothing, for charity never faileth. Wherefore, cleave unto charity, which is the greatest of all, for all things must fail –

7:47 But charity is the pure love of Christ, and it endureth forever; and whoso is found possessed of it at the last day, it shall be well with him.

7:48 Wherefore, my beloved brethren, pray unto the Father with all the energy of heart, that ye may be filled with this love, which he hath bestowed upon all who are true followers of his Son, Jesus Christ; that ye may become the sons of God; that when he shall appear we shall be like him, for we shall see him as he is; that we may have this hope; that we may be purified even as he is pure. Amen.

Moroni 10:8-16 - Moroni speaks about the gifts of the Spirit of God . . . and to another, the beholding of angels and ministering spirits

10:8 And again, I exhort you, my brethren, that ye deny not the gifts of God, for they are many; and they come from the same God. And there are different ways that these gifts are administered; but it is the same God who worketh all in all; and they are given by the manifestations of the Spirit of God unto men, to profit them.

10:9 For behold, to one is given by the Spirit of God, that he may teach the word of wisdom;

10:10 And to another, that he may teach the word of knowledge by the same Spirit;

10:11 And to another, exceedingly great faith; and to another, the gifts of healing by the same Spirit;

10:12 And again, to another, that he may work mighty miracles;

10:13 And again, to another, that he may prophesy concerning all things;

10:14 And again, to another, the beholding of <u>angels</u> and ministering spirits;

10:15 And again, to another, all kinds of tongues;

10:16 And again, to another, the interpretation of languages and of divers kinds of tongues.

Acknowledgements

Thank you -

Kay Stitzel, Sara Jess, Donna DeHaan, and Jennifer Guttersen for your editing, organizing, and proofreading skills.

Mike White, Publishing Consultant of Ghost River Images, for your talent in turning a manuscript into a beautiful book.

And, of course, the Angels for your guidance, love, and constant encouragement.

About The Author

Kermie Wohlenhaus, Ph.D. is an author, TV producer, and angelologist. She teaches workshops and classes, gives angel presentations nationally, and hosts a TV show in Tucson, Arizona on public access called *Kermie & the Angels* which is available on YouTube.

As an angel expert, Dr. Wohlenhaus is regularly interviewed on TV, radio, podcasts, and for newspapers and magazines throughout the United States. She is popular in live performances with radio and TV audiences for her knowledge and accurate angelic messages. Dr. Wohlenhaus is the Founder and Director of the School of Angel Studies.

Dr. Wohlenhaus has also authored *How to Talk and Actually Listen to Your Guardian Angel,* which is available in Spanish, French and German. *The Complete Reference to Angels in the Bible, A Quick Reference Guide to Angels in the Bible* along with *The Complete Reference to Angels in The Book of Mormon* are the first in a series by Dr. Wohlenhaus called *The Complete Reference to Angels in Sacred Texts.* Also included in this *Complete Reference* series is: *Angels in The Koran (Qur'an),* and *Angels in Other Sacred Texts.* These books are important foundation texts within the field of angelology, the study of angels.

Dr. Wohlenhaus received a Bachelor of Science (BS) from Colorado State University, a Master of Divinity (MDIV) from the Iliff School of Theology, and a Doctor of Philosophy (Ph.D.) in Religion/ Metaphysics at the College of Metaphysical Studies. She is currently living in Tucson, Arizona.

For further information: www.KermieandtheAngels.com

www.ingramcontent.com/pod-product-compliance
Lightning Source LLC
Chambersburg PA
CBHW071948100426
42736CB00042B/2509